Guided Reading Notes

Red Band
Oxford Level 2

Pets

Contents

OXFORD
UNIVERSITY PRESS

Introduction

Why is guided reading important?

Guided reading plays an important role in your whole-school provision for reading, providing opportunities for children to progress and develop the key competencies they need to become confident and skilled independent readers. Working with small groups of children, with texts closely matched to the readers' needs, guided reading is the perfect vehicle for delivering focused teaching from Reception/P1 right through to Year 6/P7. The teacher-pupil interaction also provides a valuable assessment opportunity, helping you identify exactly what each child can and can't do. Through guided reading children also encounter a world of exciting, whole books – building a community of readers who read for pleasure.

About *Project X Origins*

Project X Origins is a comprehensive, whole-school guided reading programme designed to help you teach the wide range of skills essential to ensure children progress as readers and to help nurture a love of reading.

Ensuring the key skills are covered

Project X Origins incorporates all of the key skills children need to develop to become successful and enthusiastic readers:

> **Word reading:** phonically regular and common exception words are introduced systematically in the early levels with phonic opportunities provided throughout the notes. As children progress, they are encouraged to use their decoding skills whenever they encounter new or unfamiliar words, and also to recognize how this impacts on different spelling rules.

> **Comprehension:** understanding what has been read is central to being an effective and engaged reader but comprehension is not something that comes automatically so specific strategies have been built into the notes to ensure children develop comprehension skills they can use over a range of texts:

- Previewing
- Predicting
- Activating and building prior knowledge
- Questioning
- Recalling
- Visualizing and other sensory responses
- Deducing, inferring and drawing conclusions
- Determining importance
- Synthesizing
- Empathizing
- Summarizing
- Personal response, including adopting a critical response

> **Reading fluency:** fluency occurs as children develop automatic word recognition, reading with pace and expression. Strategies to help achieve this, including meaningful opportunities for oral reading, re-reading and re-listening are provided throughout.

> **Vocabulary:** introducing new vocabulary within a meaningful context is an important element in extending children's vocabulary range, developing their reading fluency and comprehension. Each thematic cluster provides opportunities for revisiting and reinforcing vocabulary over a range of books and contexts.

> **Grammar, punctuation and spelling:** learning about language in the context of a text, rather than through a series of discrete exercises, can help make grammar, punctuation and spelling relevant and helps children make the link between grammar, punctuation and clarity of meaning, thus supporting their development as writers. Opportunities to support an in-depth look at language are provided for every book from Year I/P2 to Year 6/P7.

> **Spoken language:** talk is crucial to learning and developing their comprehension so children are given plenty of opportunities to: discuss and debate their ideas with others; justify their opinions; ask and answer questions; explore and hypothesise; summarise, describe and explain; and listen and respond to the ideas of others.

Assessment and progression in reading

Project X Origins includes a rigorous assessment spine drawn from the *Oxford Reading Criterion Scale* to ensure that you know exactly what each child can do and what they need to focus on next in order to make progress. This assessment framework, combined with the careful levelling of the Oxford Levels, will help you select the right book with the right level of challenge for each of your guided reading groups and to assess, track and monitor each child's progress.

Step 1

On a termly basis, use the *Oxford Reading Criterion Scale* (which can be found in the relevant *Project X Origins Teaching Handbook*) to assess each child's reading. The scale will tell you the Oxford Level a child is comfortable reading at, and the areas a child needs to develop. You can also use this assessment to form your guided reading groups.

Step 2

Plan your guided reading sessions by selecting books at the appropriate Oxford Level that focus on the relevant learning needs of the group. You will find charts showing the learning objectives and assessment points for every *Project X Origins* book in the relevant *Project X Origins Teaching Handbook*. Depending on your assessment, you might choose a book at the level the children are comfortable at or one from the next level up, to offer some stretch.

Step 3

Use the assessment points within the Guided Reading Notes to support on-going assessment of children's reading progress. The Progress Tracking Charts in the relevant *Project X Origins Teaching Handbook* can be used to record this if you wish. Regularly re-assess each child's progress combining your on-going informal assessments and the termly assessment using the *Oxford Reading Criterion Scale*. Use this information to re-organize guided reading groups and teaching plans in response to children's varying degrees of progress.

Getting started: using the Guided Reading Notes

At a glance

Project X Origins Guided Reading Notes offer detailed guidance to help deliver effective and engaging guided reading sessions, and are designed to be used flexibly to ensure you get the most out of each book. For notes containing multiple sessions, you may choose to focus on each of these sessions or focus on one session and have the children read the rest of the book independently.

Curricular correlation and assessment

At the beginning of every set of notes there are correlation charts for all UK curricula, ensuring that across the clusters the main curricular objectives are covered. In addition, an overview of assessment points for each book is provided – these points are also signposted throughout the notes.

Key information

Before the first session, an overview of the book and the resources you will need (such as additional photocopy masters) is provided.

Teaching sequence

Each guided reading session follows the same teaching sequence:

- **Before reading**: children explore the context of each book to support their understanding and help them engage with the text. They are encouraged to discuss, recall, respond, predict and speculate about the book. Opportunities to focus on word reading and/or vocabulary are also introduced at this point.
- **During reading**: children are given a section of the book to read with specific questions in mind.
- **After reading**: children reflect on and discuss what they have read. They are encouraged to delve deeper, exploring their understanding of the text, developing their vocabulary, grammar, punctuation, spelling and fluency where appropriate.
- **Follow-up**: opportunities for children to extend their learning outside the session are provided, including writing and cross-curricular activities.

Throughout the sessions, the key strategies that children are developing are clearly identified.

My Cat Moggy

BY TONY BRADMAN

Curricular correlation

English Early Years Foundation Stage

Speaking	Extends vocabulary, especially by grouping and narrowing, exploring the meaning and sounds of new words
	Introduces a story or narrative into their play
Reading	Can segment the sounds in simple words and blend them together and knows which letters represent some of them
	Begins to read words and simple sentences

Phonics and vocabulary

GPCs	/ee/ sees, feet, sleeps /ll/ wall, dull, tell
Decodable words (Phase 2 and 3)	is, cat, see, dig, feet, run, fun, too, much, in, wall, on, a, now, dull, sleep, garden, lands, jump, can, tell
Common exception words	you, her, she
Challenge and context words	Moggy, Tiger, leap, day, eat, one, want, story

Reading assessment points (Oxford Reading Criterion Scale: Assessment Standard I)

12.	Can the children retell familiar stories with growing confidence? (R)
19.	Can children read words with some vowel digraphs e.g. /ee/? (READ)
21.	Are the children beginning to make predictions based on titles, text, blurb and/or illustrations? (D)

Scottish Curriculum for Excellence

Listening and talking	As I listen and talk in different situations, I am learning to take turns and am developing my awareness of when to talk and when to listen LIT 0-02a / ENG 0-03a
Reading	I explore sounds, letters and words, discovering how they work together, and I can use what I learn to help me as I read and write ENG 0-12a / LIT 0-13a / LIT 0-21a
	I enjoy exploring events and characters in stories and other texts, sharing my thoughts in different ways LIT 0-19a

Foundation Phase Framework for Wales

Oracy	Contribute to role-play activities using relevant language (Speaking)
	Ask questions about something that has been said (Listening)
Reading	Recognise that words are constructed from phonemes (sounds) and that phonemes are represented by graphemes (written letters): blend combinations of letters; segment combinations of letters (Reading strategies)
	Retell familiar stories in a simple way (Comprehension)

Northern Ireland Curriculum

Talking and Listening	Offer reasons to support opinions given
	Develop language and thinking through sharing their thoughts, feelings and ideas with different audiences
Reading	Understand and use some language associated with books

About this book

Tiger thinks his cat sleeps all day but when he shrinks he sees his cat has a very busy time.

You will need

- *Sequencing pictures* Photocopy Master, *Teaching Handbook* for Reception/P1
- *Sequencing sentences* Photocopy Master, *Teaching Handbook* for Reception/P1
- Soft toy cats or puppets
- Toy figures

❯ Before reading

- Read the title of the book and look at the front cover together. Ask the children what they think the book might be about. **(predicting)** ≪ ≪ ≪ ≪ ≪

- Ask them to tell you what they know about cats and their behaviour. Ask them to give you one-word suggestions in answer to the question. Try to include the words: *sleep, leap, jump, dig, run.* **(activating prior knowledge)**

- Ask them to find the word *Moggy* on the back cover and then read the blurb to them.

Assessment point

Are the children beginning to make predictions based on titles, text, blurb and/or illustrations?
(ORCS Standard 1, 21)

⤳ *Phonic opportunity*

■ Write the action words from the story on cards so the children can see them. Make up actions to represent each word, e.g. running up and down on the spot holding a toy cat to show the word *run* and practise the actions as you point to the word. You could practise sounding out and blending some of these words if you wish.

■ Play a game. Place the action word cards on the table face down. As a child picks up a card they should enact the word with the toy cat, using the agreed action. You could also sing a refrain to go with the action, e.g. 'jump cat, jump cat, jump, jump, jump' to the tune of 'Run rabbit run'. Mix the cards up after each child's turn.

■ On a piece of paper, write the word *see*. Indicate the two graphemes in the word and demonstrate how to blend them. Draw attention to the /ee/ sound. Now look at pages 3, 6, 8, 9, 10, 11, 12 and ask the children if they can identify the word with the /ee/ sound on each page. ≪ ≪ ≪ ≪ ≪≪

■ Alternatively, depending on the phonic work you have been undertaking, select one or two of the words from the book and remind the children how to sound and blend phonemes.

> **Assessment point**
> Can children read words with some vowel digraphs e.g. /ee/? (ORCS Standard 1, 19)

❯ **During reading**

■ Depending on your usual practice and the group you are working with, you may wish to:

■ Share the book with the children before they read it themselves.

- Read the first few pages together and ask the children to read the rest independently. In this case read pages 2–3 to the children. Model pleasure in using spoken and written language, by using lots of expression. Discuss what has happened and check the children understand why Tiger thinks the cat is dull.

- Invite them to read the whole book independently.

- Ask the children to read the book quietly.

- If you have not done so already, remind the children what to do if they encounter a difficult word. Praise children who successfully decode unfamiliar words.

- As you listen to individual children read, you might want to ask them to stop and summarize what has happened so far and predict what will happen next. **(summarizing, predicting)**

After reading

Returning to the text

- You may wish to quickly re-read the story to the children to enhance their engagement and understanding. **(engaging readers)**

- Ask if they enjoyed the story. What was funny about the ending? **(personal response, inferring and deducing)**

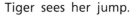
Tiger sees her jump.

Tiger sees her run!

Developing comprehension

■ Give each child a small-world figure to represent micro-Tiger. In pairs, ask the children to re-enact the story together. They can include the actions they have used earlier if they wish. **(recall, visualizing and other sensory responses)**

Tiger sees her dig.

6

Tiger sees her eat.

7

> Follow-up

Literacy activities

- Cut out the *Sequencing pictures* Photocopy Master and challenge the children to sequence the story. They could add their own marks, words or sentences to these pictures or match the pictures with a sentence from the *Sequencing sentences* Photocopy Master.

- Invite the children to make up their own Tiger and cat stories using the toy cat/small-world figure. They could draw pictures of their stories, using divided paper to encourage a storyboard approach and/or use the 'clip art' assets in the Project X *Interactive Stories* software to tell their own stories.

- Encourage the children to make up a story about a cat using a pet name of their choosing. Invite children to share their stories with each other.

- Encourage the children to reread the book - individually and to other children or adults.

- Sing other action rhymes and cat related nursery rhymes such as 'Pussy cat, pussy cat where have you been?'

Other activities

- Challenge children to make up their own action game to play in the outdoor area. They could create a refrain to go with each action.

- Help children to make a simple bar chart showing pets owned by class members.

Pickles' New Home
BY SHOO RAYNER

Curricular correlation

English Early Years Foundation Stage

Speaking	Uses talk to organise, sequence and clarify thinking, ideas, feelings and events
Reading	Can segment the sounds in simple words and blend them together and knows which letters represent some of them
	Begins to read words and simple sentences

Phonics and vocabulary

GPCs	/**ow**/ down, now, wow
Decodable words (Phase 2 and 3)	has, in, Ant, Cat, can, this, up, tell, now, down, wow, spin, fall, sleep
Common exception words	the, you, go, are, to
Challenge and context words	Pickles, dizzy, home, time, new

Reading assessment points (Oxford Reading Criterion Scale: Assessment Standard 1)

20.	Can the children talk about main points or key events in a simple text? (R)
21.	Are the children beginning to make predictions based on titles, text, blurb and/or illustrations? (D)
25.	Can the children confidently sound and blend words containing taught vowel and consonant digraphs? (READ)

Scottish Curriculum for Excellence

Listening and talking	I enjoy exploring events and characters in stories and other texts, sharing my thoughts in different ways LIT 0-01c
Reading	I enjoy exploring events and characters in stories and other texts, sharing my thoughts in different ways LIT 0-19a
	To help me understand stories and other texts, I ask questions and link what I am learning with what I already know LIT 0-07a / LIT 0-16a / ENG 0-17a

Foundation Phase Framework for Wales

Oracy	Talk about things from their experience and share information (Speaking)
Reading	Relate information and ideas from a text to personal experience (Comprehension)
	Apply the following reading strategies with support: phonic strategies to decode simple words; recognition of high-frequency words; context clues; repetition in texts (Reading strategies)

Northern Ireland Curriculum

Talking and Listening	Develop social use of language through initiating and joining in conversations in pairs or groups
Reading	Share a range of books with adults/other pupils

<table>
<tr><td>

About this book

Ant and Cat shrink and have fun playing in the hamster's new cage.

</td><td>

You will need

- *Up/down/spin round* Photocopy Master, *Teaching Handbook* for Reception/PI
- *Sequencing* Photocopy Master, *Teaching Handbook* for Reception/PI
- A hamster cage and/or hamster if possible

</td></tr>
</table>

❯ Before reading

- If you have a hamster/hamster cage show these to the children and invite them to talk about what they know about hamsters and their behaviour. Discuss what the hamster does with the wheel, tubes and levels of the cage if your cage has these items. Look at the picture of Pickles' cage on page 3 and look for these features. **(activating prior knowledge, engaging readers)**

- Look at page 2 and identify the characters and the name of the hamster. Point out the word *Pickles* in the title and on pages 2, 3, 4 and I3. **(activating prior knowledge, developing vocabulary)**

> **Assessment point**
>
> Are the children beginning to make predictions based on titles, text, blurb and/or illustrations?
> (ORCS Standard I, 2I)

- Look at the front and back cover and talk about what the story might be about. **(predicting)**

- Write the words *up*, *down* and *spin* so the children can see them. Point to them randomly. Say the word and ask the children to repeat it as they stand up, sit down or turn around, as appropriate. Repeat this several times. You could let one of the children select and read the words for the others to enact. **(developing vocabulary)**

→ *Phonic opportunity*

- On a piece of paper, write the word *how*. Indicate the two graphemes in the word and demonstrate how to blend them. Draw attention to the /ow/ sound. Now look at pages 8 and 11 and ask the children if they can identify the word with the /ow/ sound on each page. ≪≪≪≪≪≪

- Alternatively, depending on the phonic work you have been undertaking, select one or two of the words from the book and remind the children how to sound and blend phonemes.

Assessment point

Can the children confidently sound and blend words containing taught vowel and consonant digraphs? (ORCS Standard 1, 25)

Now Cat can spin.

❯ During reading

- ◼ Depending on your usual practice and the group you are working with, you may wish to:
  - ☐ Share the book with the children before they read it themselves.
  - ☐ Read the first few pages together and ask the children to read the rest independently. In this case read pages 3 and 4 to the children. Model pleasure in using spoken and written language, by using lots of expression. Look at page 5 together and ask the children to speculate what Ant and Cat will do now they have shrunk.
  - ☐ Invite them to read the whole book independently.
- ◼ If you have not already done so, remind the children what to do if they encounter a difficult word. Praise children who decode unfamiliar words successfully.
- ◼ As you listen to individual children read, you might want to ask them to stop and summarize what has happened so far and predict what will happen next. **(summarizing, predicting)**
- ◼ Ask them to look out for the words *up*, *down* and *spin*.

Now Cat and Ant can go in!

Ant can go up.

After reading

Returning to the text

- Ask the children if they enjoyed the story and what they liked about it. **(personal response)**
- Ask them what they think it would be like to be able to shrink. What would they do if they were small? **(personal response)**
- Use pages 14–15 to get children to retell the story. **(recall)**
- Ask them what they think Pickles might say to Ant and Cat if he saw them in his home (and if he could talk)? **(empathizing)**

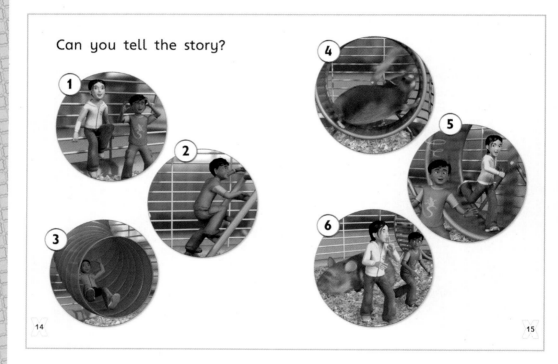

Can you tell the story?

14

15

> Follow-up

Literacy activities

- Use the *Sequencing* Photocopy Master and cut it up to sequence the story, or use it as a storyboard for children to write the story in sequence.

- Use the *Up/down/spin* Photocopy Master and ask the children to draw appropriate pictures and write captions, e.g. climb up a ladder, come downstairs, go round on a roundabout.

- Sing 'up/down/spin/round' songs and say nursery rhymes such as 'Here we go round the mulberry bush', 'Incy Wincy Spider'. Challenge children to invent and write their own versions, e.g. 'Micro, micro Ant, climbing up the tube'.

- Encourage the children to use the hamster cage and small world figures to re-enact and extend the story.

- Encourage the children to reread the book – individually and to other children or adults.

- Watch the story on the Project X *Interactive Stories* software.

Other activities

- Working with an adult, encourage the children to spin round and round to discover what happens. Ask them to describe the sensations they feel.

- Use construction toys to build a structure for hamsters or other pets to climb/play on.

- Use outdoor blocks to build an 'up/down/spin' play circuit in the outside play space. They could draw a map of their circuit.

Paco's Pet

BY DAMIAN HARVEY

Curricular correlation

English Early Years Foundation Stage

Speaking	Uses talk to organise, sequence and clarify thinking, ideas, feelings and events
Reading	Can segment the sounds in simple words and blend them together and knows which letters represent some of them
	Begins to read words and simple sentences

Phonics and vocabulary

GPCs	/**ow**/ down /**th**/ this, that
Decodable words (Phase 2 and 3)	can, pet, not, this, as, put, zoo, it, get, back, down, lots, of, feed, that
Common exception words	you, have, no, I, put
Challenge and context words	animals, children

Reading assessment points (Oxford Reading Criterion Scale: Assessment Standard 1)

2. Can the children understand the terms: book, cover? (READ)
18. With support, can the children find information to help answer simple, literal questions? (R)
24. Can the children read most common CVC words automatically, without the need for sounding and blending? (READ)

Scottish Curriculum for Excellence

Listening and talking	I listen or watch for useful or interesting information and I use this to make choices or learn new things LIT 0-04a
Reading	I use signs, books or other texts to find useful or interesting information and I use this to plan, make choices or learn new things LIT 0-14a

Foundation Phase Framework for Wales

Oracy	Contribute to role-play activities using relevant language (Speaking)
Reading	Read simple words such as consonant-vowel-consonant words (Reading strategies)
	Recognise and make meaning from words and pictures on-screen (Reading strategies)

Northern Ireland Curriculum

Talking and Listening	Develop an extended vocabulary through listening and responding to adults and peers
Reading	Read with some independence
	Use extended vocabulary when discussing text, retelling stories or in emergent writing

About this book

Paco wants a pet but his mum keeps saying *no!*.

You will need

- *Sequencing pictures* Photocopy Master, *Teaching Handbook* for Reception/P1
- *Is it a good pet?* Photocopy Master, *Teaching Handbook* for Reception/P1
- Small-world zoo and farm animals

> Before reading

- Read the title of the book and look at the front cover together. Ask the children what they think the book might be about. **(predicting)** ≪≪≪

- Ask them to tell you about any visits they have made to zoos or safari parks and what they saw there. Alternatively, you could show a brief video clip on a whiteboard to stimulate talk. **(activating prior knowledge)**

- Give the children a handful of toy animals – some farm animals and some pets. Have two hoops on the table labelled Pets/Not Pets. In turns, children should put one of the animals in one of the hoops and say why they think it belongs in that group. Talk about why some animals would not be good pets (size, not used to people, need special food, need lots of looking after). **(activating prior knowledge, engaging readers)**

Assessment point

Can the children understand the terms: book, cover?
(ORCS Standard 1, 2)

Phonic opportunity

- On a piece of paper, write the word *this*. Ask the children to identify the different sounds in the word. Draw attention to the digraph. Now look at pages 5, 7, 9, 11 and 13 with the children. Ask them to find and read words with the digraph th in them.

- Alternatively, depending on the phonic work you have been undertaking, select one or two of the words from the book and remind the children how to sound and blend phonemes.

- If needed, go over any common exception words such as: *have, you*.

No you can not.

Can I have this as a pet?

> During reading

- Depending on your usual practice and the group you are working with, you may wish to:
  - ☐ Share the book with the children before they read it themselves.
  - ☐ Read the first few pages together and ask the children to read the rest independently. In this case look at page 2 and read page 3 to the children. Ask why they think Paco is asking for a pet. What do they think Mum will say? Why? Then ask them to read on independently.
  - ☐ Invite them to read the whole book independently.
- If you have not done so already, remind the children what to do if they encounter a difficult word. Praise children who can successfully decode unfamiliar words.
- As you listen to individual children read, you might want to ask them to stop and summarize what has happened so far and predict what will happen next. **(summarizing, predicting)**

After reading

Returning to the text

- You may wish to quickly reread the story to the children to enhance their engagement and understanding. **(engaging readers)**

- Ask if they enjoyed the story and what was funny about the ending. **(personal response, inferring, deducing)**.

- Ask who the main people in the story are. How does it start? How does it end? **(recall, determining importance)**

Assessment point

With support, can the children find information to help answer simple, literal questions? (ORCS Standard 1, 18)

- If Mum had said *yes*, which of the animals selected by Paco could have been pets? Which could not have been pets? **(prior knowledge, inferring and deducing)**

- Why do they think Mum kept saying *no*? **(empathizing)**

Developing fluency

- Encourage the children to reread the book – individually and to other children or adults. Get them to use lots of expression for the *No you can not* part.

Assessment point

Can the children read most common CVC words automatically, without the need for sounding and blending? (ORCS Standard 1, 24)

Can I have a pet?

No!
Put it down.

> Follow-up

Literacy activities

- Cut up the *Sequencing pictures* Photocopy Master and invite the children to sequence the story. They could add their own marks, words or sentences to these pictures.

- Challenge the children to make up oral zoo stories while playing with small-world animals. Some could then draw pictures of their stories, using divided paper to encourage a storyboard approach, or they could make a storyboard using digital pictures of scenes they have set up.

Other activities

- Use the *Is it a good pet?* Photocopy Master and ask the children to sort animals into good pets/not good pets. Encourage them to label or list the animals in each column.

- Ask the children to make up their own song about choosing a pet. They could use the following pattern: 'I chose a .... Mum said NO.' The final verse could be: 'Then I chose a ... and Mum said YES'.

A Dog's Day
BY CLAIRE LLEWELLYN

Curricular correlation

English Early Years Foundation Stage

Speaking	Uses talk to organise, sequence and clarify thinking, ideas, feelings and events
Reading	Can segment the sounds in simple words and blend them together and knows which letters represent some of them
	Knows that information can be retrieved from books and computers

Phonics and vocabulary

GPCs	/**oo**/ food /**ee**/ been, sleep /**sh**/ wash
Decodable words (Phase 2 and 3)	dog, Pip, is, then, ball, has, this, food, with, been, runs, sleep, pond, jump
Common exception words	she, her
Challenge and context words	drink, busy, day, wash

Reading assessment points (Oxford Reading Criterion Scale: Assessment Standard 1)

9.	Do the children know information can be retrieved from different sources such as books? (R)
15.	Can the children read words with consonant digraphs? ch, sh, th, ng? (READ)
18.	With support, can the children find information to help answer simple, literal questions? (R)

Scottish Curriculum for Excellence

Listening and talking	I listen or watch for useful or interesting information and I use this to make choices or learn new things LIT 0-04a
Reading	I use signs, books or other texts to find useful or interesting information and I use this to plan, make choices or learn new things LIT 0-14a

Foundation Phase Framework for Wales

Oracy	Ask questions about something that has been said (Listening)
Reading	Read simple captions and texts recognising high-frequency words (Reading strategies)
	Show an interest in books and other reading materials and respond to their content (Response and analysis)

Northern Ireland Curriculum

Talking and Listening	Answer questions to give information and demonstrate understanding
	Ask questions to find information or seek an explanation
Reading	Browse and choose books for a specific purpose

About this book

This book gives information about what a dog needs to stay healthy and happy.

You will need

- *Pip's day* Photocopy Master, *Teaching Handbook* for Reception/PI
- Tin of dog food, a water bowl and food bowl
- Examples of dog-care products such as collar and lead and toys
- Pictures of dogs

❯ Before reading

- Read the title of the book and look at the front and back cover together. Ask the children to tell you what they know about what dogs usually do in an ordinary day. Talk about how a dog needs food, water, play and exercise to be healthy, just like other pets – and us. It also needs someone to look after it and care for it, just like other pets – and us. **(activating prior knowledge)**

- Turn through the pages and look at the pictures to see what sort of things Pip does and introduce the words: *sleep, jump, wash* and *drink*. **(previewing the text, engaging readers)**

- Hand round the food packages, feeding bowls and other dog-care items. Ask when Pip might need any of the dog care items you have looked at. **(activating prior knowledge)**

Phonic opportunity

- On a piece of paper, write the word *that*. Ask the children to identify the different sounds in the word. Draw attention to the digraph. Now look at pages 2, 5, 6, 7, 9, 10, 11 and 13 with the children. Ask them to find and read words with the digraph 'th' in them.

- Alternatively, depending on the phonic work you have been undertaking, select one or two of the words from the book and remind the children how to sound out and blend phonemes.

Assessment point

Can the children read words with consonant digraphs? ch, sh, th, ng? (ORCS Standard I, 15)

During reading

- Depending on your usual practice and the group you are working with, you may wish to:
  - ☐ Share the book with the children before they read it themselves.
  - ☐ Read the first few pages together and ask the children to read the rest independently. In this case, read pages 2–3 to the children and read pages 4–5 together. Then ask them to read the book independently.
  - ☐ Invite them to read the whole book independently.
- If you have not done so already, remind children what to do if they encounter a difficult word. Praise children who successfully decode unfamiliar words.
- As they read ask them to be thinking about all the things the dog needs to be happy and healthy.

Jump Pip!

Pip jumps in the pond.

Then she has a sleep.

8

9

> After reading

Returning to the text

- You may wish to quickly reread the book to the children to enhance their engagement and understanding. **(engaging readers)**

- Ask them if this book is a story about a dog or if it tells you something else (the kinds of things a dog does in a day/what it needs to be healthy). Discuss their ideas about fiction/non-fiction texts. This may include the type of illustrations. ❰❰❰❰

> **Assessment point**
> Do the children know information can be retrieved from different sources such as books? (ORCS Standard I, 9)

- Ask them what things the book shows them that dogs need in order to be happy and healthy. Do they think there is anything else? **(recall, inferring)**

- Ask them where there is a list to show them all the things that Pip does. **(locating information)**

- Use pages 14–15 to prompt recall of Pip's activities. Ask the children to match the pictures on pages 14–15 to the pages of the book. **(recall, locating information)** ❰

> **Assessment point**
> With support, can the children find information to help answer simple, literal questions? (ORCS Standard I, 18)

It has been a busy day!

❯ Follow-up

Literacy activities

- Use pages 14–15 to encourage the children to write a sentence saying what Pip is doing in each picture.
- Invite children to write their own pet care list for their own pet/class pet.
- Use the *Pip's Day* Photocopy Master to match the activities to the appropriate word.
- Challenge children to create their own picture-based information book about a dog's day (or a typical day in the life of any other pet).

Other activities

- If they have read *My Cat Moggy*, ask what they remember about what cats do in a day. Ask how are cats and dogs alike? How are they different?
- Encourage the children to roleplay using the dog care items and soft toys of dogs.
- Have a collection of pictures of dogs and ask the children to sort these and explain their criteria for sorting, e.g. size, colour, breed, activity.
- Make up a song or action rhyme about a dog's day. Children could use the pattern 'At eight o'clock we ... feed our pet, feed our pet, feed our pet' and so on to the tune of 'This is the way we wash our face ...'

My Pet
BY MONICA HUGHES

Curricular correlation

English Early Years Foundation Stage

Speaking	Uses talk to organise, sequence and clarify thinking, ideas, feelings and events
Reading	Can segment the sounds in simple words and blend them together and knows which letters represent some of them
	Knows that information can be retrieved from books and computers

Phonics and vocabulary

GPCs	/**th**/ thin /**sh**/ fish /**ng**/ long
Decodable words (Phase 2 and 3)	pet, cat, dog, can, fish, see, long, thin, hamster, it, in, rabbit, cockatoo
Common exception words	my, you, me, are, to
Challenge and context words	lives, talk, cage, snake, many, baby

Reading assessment points (Oxford Reading Criterion Scale: Assessment Standard 1)

6. Can the children read some words from the YR/P1 high frequency word list? (READ)
15. Can the children read words with consonant digraphs: ch, sh, th, ng? (READ)
18. With support, can the children find information to help answer simple, literal questions? (R)

Scottish Curriculum for Excellence

Listening and talking	To help me understand stories and other texts, I ask questions and link what I am learning with what I already know LIT 0-07a / LIT 0-16a / ENG 0-17a
Reading	To help me understand stories and other texts, I ask questions and link what I am learning with what I already know LIT 0-07a / LIT 0-16a / ENG 0-17a
	I use signs, books or other texts to find useful or interesting information and I use this to plan, make choices or learn new things LIT 0-14a

Foundation Phase Framework for Wales

Oracy	Talk about things from their experience and share information (Speaking)
Reading	Show an awareness of the difference between stories and information texts (Reading strategies)
	Make meaning from visual features of the text, e.g. illustrations, photographs, diagrams and charts (Reading strategies)

Northern Ireland Curriculum

Talking and Listening	Answer questions to give information and demonstrate understanding
	Ask questions to find information or seek an explanation
Reading	Listen to a range of stories, poems and non-fiction text read to them by adults/other pupils
	Understand the purpose and use of environmental print

About this book

This book explores different pets. It includes a pet graph.

You will need

- *Pet tally chart* Photocopy Master, *Teaching Handbook* for Reception/P1
- *Pet-homes* Photocopy Master, *Teaching Handbook* for Reception/P1
- Small-world animals
- Pictures of pet homes, e.g. rabbit hutch, bird cage, cat basket, dog kennel, fish tank, stable, hamster cage

> Before reading

- Read the title of the book and look at the front and back cover together. Ask them to talk about any pets they or their families have. List what these are. **(activating prior knowledge)**
- Show the children pictures of pet homes and discuss the names or ask if any of their pets have special homes. List the answers under the appropriate pictures, e.g. cage, hutch, tank. **(activating prior knowledge)**
- Play a game. Point to the home and say its name. Children have to make an appropriate noise or action (agreed beforehand) for the animal that lives there, e.g. woof for a dog, puff out cheeks for a hamster, twitch nose for a rabbit. After a few turns, you make the noise/action and the children must touch the appropriate picture and say the word, e.g. *kennel*.

⤳ *Phonic opportunity*

- ◾ Find the words *long*, *thin* and *fish* in the book. Ask the children to identify the diagraphs, then read the words by sounding and blending the phonemes. ⟨⟨

- ◾ Write the word *cockatoo*, putting a slash between the syllables. Sound-talk the first syllable and blend it. Do the same for the other syllables. Say all three syllables. Repeat and ask the children to join in. Now look at page 12 of the book. Point to the word *cockatoo* and blend each syllable. Explain that a cockatoo is a type of bird.

Assessment point

Can the children read words with consonant digraphs: ch, sh, th, ng? (ORCS Standard 1, 15)

Fish

My pets are fish.
How many fish can you see?

14

15

> During reading

- Depending on your usual practice and the group you are working with, you may wish to:

  - ☐ Share the book with the children before they read it themselves.

  - ☐ Read the first few pages together and ask the children to read the rest independently. In this case look at pages 2–3 together and then read pages 4–5 together. Discuss the pages, pointing out the function of the page headings and then ask them to carry on reading independently. ≪ ≪

  - ☐ Invite them to read the whole book independently.

- If you have not done so already, remind the children what to do if they encounter a difficult word. Praise children who successfully decode unfamiliar words.

> **Assessment point**
>
> Can the children read some words from the YR/ PI high frequency word list?
> (ORCS Standard I, 6)

Snake

My pet is a snake.

10

It is long and thin.

11

After reading

Returning to the text

- You may wish to quickly reread the book to the children to enhance their engagement and understanding. **(engaging readers)**

- Discuss any comments and questions they might have. **(personal response, questioning)**

- Ask some 'who' and 'where' questions: who lives in a ...?, Where does an X live ...?
  Ask the children to show you the answer in the book. **(recall, locating information)**

- Discuss whether this is a factual book or a story book. How do they know?

- Ask them to show you which page heading and picture tells them what the page is about: birds, fish and so on. **(locating information)** ≪≪≪≪≪≪

> **Assessment point**
> With support, can the children find information to help answer simple, literal questions?
> (ORCS Standard I, 18)

> Follow-up

Literacy activities

- Use the Pet homes Photocopy Master and get the children to cut out and match the pets to their homes. Encourage them to write a sentence under each completed match. You could model the writing pattern: *A ... lives in a ....*
- Write a sentence or two about their own pet.

Other activities

- Look at the graph on page 16 together and discuss how this information could be collected. Use the Pet tally chart Photocopy Master to get the children to write types of pets and then undertake (or role play undertaking) a survey of class pets. They must approach other children politely, explain what they are doing and listen carefully to the answer.
- Make a class bar chart of pets.
- Adapt the song 'Old McDonald had a farm' to become 'Old McDonald had a pet'.
- Encourage the children to role play using the small-world animals and/or animal soft toys.
- Encourage the children to make a model home for a pet of their choice.